Editor
Eric Migliaccio

Managing Editor
Ina Massler Levin, M.A.

Editor-in-Chief
Sharon Coan, M.S. Ed.

Illustrator
Howard Chaney

Cover Artist
Brenda DiAntonis

Art Coordinator
Kevin Barnes

Imaging
Rosa C. See

Product Manager
Phil Garcia

Publisher
Mary D. Smith, M.S. Ed.

W9-AZY-284

Nonfiction Reading Comprehension

Grade 5

Geography

Science

History

Includes Standards & Benchmarks

Author

Debra J. Housel, M.S. Ed.

Teacher Created Resources

Teacher Created Resources, Inc.
6421 Industry Way
Westminster, CA 92683
www.teachercreated.com

ISBN: 978-0-7439-3385-8

©2003 Teacher Created Resources, Inc.
Reprinted, 2008
Made in U.S.A.

Table of Contents

Introduction

Comprehension is the primary goal of any reading task. Students who comprehend expository text will have more opportunities in life, as well as better test performance. Through the use of nonfiction passages followed by exercises that require vital reading and thinking skills, *Nonfiction Reading Comprehension* will help you to develop confident readers and strengthen the comprehension skills necessary for a lifetime of learning.

Each passage in *Nonfiction Reading Comprehension* covers a grade-level appropriate curriculum topic in geography, history, and science. The activities are time-efficient, allowing students to practice these skills often. To yield the best results, such practice must begin during the second quarter or when a solid majority of your class can read independently at a fifth-grade level.

✛ Essential Comprehension Skills

The questions following each passage in *Nonfiction Reading Comprehension* appear in the same order and cover seven vital skills:

✧ Locating facts

Questions based on exactly what the text states: *who, what, when, where, why,* and *how many*

✧ Identifying sequence

Questions based on chronological order: what happened first, last, and in between

✧ Noting conditions

Questions that ask students to identify similarities and differences, as well as cause-and-effect relationships

✧ Understanding vocabulary in context

Questions based on the ability to infer word meaning from the syntax and semantics of the surrounding text, as well as the ability to recognize known synonyms and antonyms for a newly encountered word

✧ Making inferences

Questions that require students to evaluate, to make decisions, and to draw logical conclusions

✧ Integrating knowledge

Questions that ask readers to draw upon their visualization skills combined with prior knowledge (These questions reinforce the crucial skill of picturing the text.)

✧ Supporting answers

A short-answer question at the end of each passage that helps students to personalize knowledge, state an opinion, and support it.

Meeting Standards and Benchmarks

Every passage in *Nonfiction Reading Comprehension* and its comprehension questions cover one or more of these language arts standards:

Reading	Writing
• Makes and revises predictions about text	• Writes compound sentences
• Uses prior knowledge to understand new information presented in text	• Follows conventions of capitalization, spelling, and punctuation appropriate for grade level
• Visualizes what is read	• Uses adjectives, adverbs, and pronouns to make writing diverse and interesting
• Uses context clues to decode unknown words	• Adheres to grammatical and mechanical conventions in writing
• Monitors own reading and independently takes action to increase understanding (self-corrects, rereads, slows down if necessary)	• States an opinion and supports it in writing
• Understands the main idea of nonfiction text	
• Integrates new information into personal knowledge base	
• Draws conclusions and makes inferences about information in the text	
• Develops ideas, opinions, and personal responses to what is read	

At the top of each passage appears the specific McREL content area standard and benchmark. Used with permission from McREL (Copyright 2000 McREL, Mid-continent Research for Education and Learning. Telephone: 303-337-0990. Web site: www.mcrel.org)

✚ Readability

All of the passages have a 5.0–5.9 reading level based on the Flesch Kincaid Readability Formula. This formula, which is built into Microsoft Word, determines a readability level by calculating the number of words, syllables, and sentences. Although content area terms can be challenging, students can handle difficult words within the context given. The passages are presented in order of increasing difficulty within each content area.

✚ Preparing Students to Read Nonfiction Text

Prepare your students to read the passages in *Nonfiction Reading Comprehension* by daily reading aloud a short nonfiction selection from another source. Reading expository text aloud is critical to developing your students' ability to read it themselves. Since making predictions is a good way to help students to understand nonfiction, read the beginning of a passage, then stop and ask them to predict what might occur next. Do this at several points throughout your reading of the text. Talking about nonfiction concepts is also very important. Remember, however, that discussion can never replace reading aloud because people rarely speak using the vocabulary and complex sentence structures of written language.

How to Use this Book

If you have some students who cannot read the articles independently, allow them to read with a partner, then work through the comprehension questions alone. As soon as possible, move to having all students practice reading and answering the questions independently.

✤ Multiple-Choice Questions

Do the first two passages and related questions on pages 8–11 with the whole class. These passages have the most challenging reading level because you will do them together. Demonstrate your own cognitive processes by thinking aloud about how to figure out an answer. This means that you tell your students your thoughts as they come to you. Let's say that this is a passage your class has read:

> Years ago, 100,000 grizzly bears lived in the United States. Now there are only about 1,000 (not including those that live in Alaska). In 1975 a law was passed to keep people from hunting the bears or destroying their homes. So today there are many more bears than in 1975. Almost all of them live in Yellowstone National Park. Sometimes the bears leave the park and kill cows or sheep. Some people feel afraid. They want to be able to shoot any grizzly that leaves the park. But others say that the bear population is already too small. They do not want the law changed.

Following the reading, one of the questions is: "In Yellowstone National Park, grizzly bears a) live in cages, b) can do tricks, c) get caught in traps, or d) wander freely." Tell the students your thoughts as they occur to you: "Well, the article said that the bears sometimes leave the park, so they must not be in cages. So I'll eliminate that choice. They are wild bears, so I doubt that they do any tricks. That leaves me with the choices 'get caught in traps' or 'wander around.' Let me look back at the article and see what it says about traps." (Refer back to article.) "I don't see anything about traps in the passage. And I did see that there is a law to keep the bears safe. That means they're safe from traps, which are dangerous. So I'm going to select 'd) wander freely.'"

The fourth question is about vocabulary. Teach students to substitute the word choices for the vocabulary term (bolded) in the passage. For each choice they should ask, "Does this make sense?" This will help them to identify the best choice.

Teach students to look for the key words in a response or question and search for those specific words in the text. Explain that they may need to look for synonyms for the key words. When you go over the practice passages, ask your students to show where they found the correct response in the text.

How to Use this Book (cont.)

✤ Short-Answer Questions

The short-answer question for each passage is an opinion statement with no definitive right answer. Each student makes a statement and explains it. While there is no correct response, it is critical to show them how to support their opinions using facts and logic. Show them a format for response: reword the question as a statement that includes their opinion followed by the word "because" and a reason. Here's a good student response: "I do not think that whales should be kept at sea parks because they are wild animals. They want to be in the ocean with their herd. It's wrong to take animals from their native habitats and train them to do tricks for our enjoyment."

Do not award credit unless the student adequately supports his or her conclusion. Before passing back the practice papers, make note of two students with opposing opinions. Then, during the discussion, call on each of these students to read his or her short-answer response to the class. If all your students drew the same conclusion or had the same opinion, come up with support for the opposing one yourself.

For the most effective practice sessions, follow these six steps:

1. Have students read the text silently and answer the questions.
2. Collect all the papers to score them.
3. Return the papers to the students and discuss how they determined their answers.
4. Point out how students had to use their background knowledge to answer certain questions.
5. Call on at least two students with different viewpoints to read and discuss their responses to the short-answer question.
6. Have your students complete the achievement bar graph on page 7, showing how many questions they answered correctly for each practice passage. Seeing their scores improve or stay consistently high over time will provide encouragement and motivation.

Scoring the Passages

Since the passages are meant as skill builders, do not include the passage scores in students' class grades. With the students, use the "number correct" approach to scoring the practice passages, especially since this coincides with the student achievement graph. However, for your own records and to share with the parents, you may want to keep a track of numeric scores for each student. If you choose to do this, do not write the numeric score on the paper. To generate a numeric score, follow these guidelines:

Multiple Choice questions (6)	15 points each	90 points
Short Answer question (1)	10 points	10 points
Total		**100 points**

✤ Practice Makes Perfect

The more your students practice, the more competent and confident they will become. Plan to have your class do every exercise in *Nonfiction Reading Comprehension*. If you do so, you'll be pleased with your students' improved comprehension of any expository text—within your classroom and beyond its walls.

Achievement Graph

Number Correct

Passage	1	2	3	4	5	6	7
"The Inventions of Ancient China"		▨					
"Unseen Volcanoes Build New Land"							
"Changing with the Environment"							
"Niagara Falls: A Changing Natural Wonder"							
"The Amazing World Beneath Our Feet"							
"Your Remarkable Body"							
"Wild Weather"							
"A Man Concerned with Safety"							
"Nature's Recycling"							
"El Niño Brings Weird Weather"							
"Staying in Balance"							
"Changing the Chinchilla"							
"The Mighty Redwood"							
"We Need Wetlands"							
"Communicating Then and Now							
"Visiting the Moon"							
"World War II Submarines"							
"The Sky's the Limit!"							
"Working for the Right to Work"							
"Sacagawea Helped Explore America"							

History Standard: Understands selected attributes and historical developments of societies in Africa, the Americas, Asia, and Europe

Benchmark: Knows significant historical achievements of various cultures of the world

The Inventions of Ancient China

Long before digital clocks, people had mechanical clocks. A Buddhist monk named Yi Xing made the first one. In China in 725 A.D., he **devised** a clock that ran by waterwheel. He put cups on each blade of the wheel. Water poured into the first cup. It always took the same amount of time to fill each cup. Once the cup filled, its weight was too heavy for the pin that held it in place. The pin moved. This pressed a lever, and the wheel went forward one notch. Then a new cup filled up. When the cup reached the basin of water at the bottom, it emptied. As the wheel moved, it made rods and gears move, telling the time. More than 300 years later, Su Song made a similar clock. It ran for 50 years. His clock had a waterwheel that made different figures appear at the window of its five-story building. Each figure stood for a certain hour.

Mechanical clocks aren't the only important Chinese invention. Ancient China was an advanced civilization. Its people created a number of things hundreds of years before the people in Europe did. Over time, Europeans have received the credit for many of these things. For example, the Chinese actually made the first magnetic compass. They

made the fishing reel 1,400 years before anyone else. Wheelbarrows, matches, and umbrellas all came from ancient China. The Western world did not know about these things for a long time. Few people traveled between Europe and China. It was a long, hard, dangerous trip. The Himalayas, the highest mountain range in the world, separated China from the rest of the continent. In the 13th century the famous explorer Marco Polo spent 24 years in China. When he returned home, he told Europeans about the amazing things he saw there. Almost no one believed him!

Paper and gunpowder are probably the best known of the ancient Chinese inventions. They had paper as early as 200 A.D. They started using paper money 700 years later, about the same time that they invented gunpowder. However, in more recent centuries, the Chinese have not made as many advances. Most modern inventions have come from Europe, North America, and Japan.

900

1201 1202

The Inventions of Ancient China

Comprehension Questions

1. **What didn't Su Song's clock have?**

   (a) a clock face

   (b) a five-story building

   (c) figures that showed through windows

   (d) a waterwheel

2. **On a historical time line, what happened second?**

   (a) Su Song made a clock.

   (b) The Chinese invented gun powder.

   (c) Yi Xing made a clock.

   (d) The Chinese made paper.

3. **When did the Chinese invent gunpowder?**

   (a) 200 A.D.

   (b) 700 A.D.

   (c) 725 A.D.

   (d) 900 A.D.

4. **Another word for *devised* is**

   (a) discovered.

   (b) invented.

   (c) located.

   (d) broke.

5. **Why did so few people believe Marco Polo?** Inference

   (a) Few people had ever been to China, so no one could support his stories.

   (b) Because Marco Polo was a known liar.

   (c) Because Marco Polo wrote science fiction novels.

   (d) No one believed that China even existed.

6. **Picture a group of people listening to Marco Polo tell about the marvels of China. What is the look on their faces?**

   (a) boredom

   (b) fear

   (c) anger

   (d) amazement

7. **Which Chinese invention mentioned in the passage was the most important? Explain.**

   I think that the clock invention was the most important. I that the clock was important because now people need to know the time so the need a clock to tell them.

Science Standard: Understands basic Earth processes

Benchmark: Knows how features on the Earth's surface are constantly changed by a combination of slow and rapid processes (e.g., weathering; erosion; and deposition of sediment caused by waves, wind, water, and ice)

Unseen Volcanoes Build New Land

No one has ever seen some of the biggest volcanoes in the world. In fact, the Mid-Ocean Ridge is the largest mountain range on Earth. It's almost 500 miles (805 km) wide and over 30,000 miles (48,280 km) long. So why don't we see these volcanoes? They lie 1.5 miles (2.4 km) below the sea's surface!

The Mid-Ocean Ridge zigzags all over the ocean floor. Every day at least one of its volcanoes erupts. Hot lava comes out onto the sea floor. The ocean's cold water rapidly cools the lava. It turns into igneous rock. Layers of lava build up. When they reach the ocean's surface, they form a volcanic island. Hawaii and Iceland are volcanic islands. Hawaii is still growing. Its active volcanoes continue to erupt, and the lava adds more land.

The world's newest volcanic island appeared in 1963 near Iceland. Sailors on a ship saw a huge cloud of smoke and steam rising from the ocean. They went closer to see what was happening. What they saw was the birth of Surtsey, a new island. This island kept growing as more lava flowed for the next three and a half years. When the eruption ended, Surtsey was 560 feet (171 m) above sea level and a mile (1.6 km) wide.

Even the cooled lava that doesn't reach the sea's surface changes land. Over millions of years the lava that has built up on the ocean floor expands. This pushes on the continents. They move around **minutely**. Each one moves from one to three inches (2.5–7.6 cm) a year. This means that the Earth's surface constantly changes. A million years ago, the Earth looked much different than it does today. A million years from now, it will have changed again.

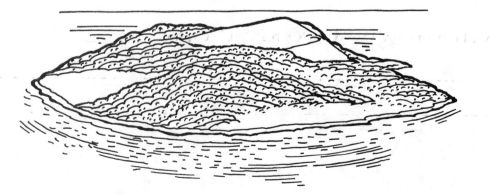

Unseen Volcanoes Build New Land

Comprehension Questions

1. **The world's newest volcanic island appeared**

    (a) in the center of the Mid-Ocean Ridge.　　(c) 500 miles west of Hawaii.

    (b) near Iceland.　　(d) next to the island of Surtsey.

2. **During the birth of Surtsey, what happened last?**

    (a) An volcano erupted under the sea.

    (b) A new island appeared in the ocean.

    (c) Clouds of steam came out of the water.

    (d) Lava cooled, forming igneous rocks.

3. **How are Hawaii and Iceland similar?**

    (a) They both have tropical climates.

    (b) The are both in the Atlantic Ocean.

    (c) They both belong to the U.S.A.

    (d) They are both volcanic islands.

4. **Another word for *minutely* is**

    (a) slightly.　　(c) up.

    (b) quickly.　　(d) down.

5. **Besides volcanoes, what other natural event changes Earth's physical features?**

    (a) forest fires　　(c) tornadoes

    (b) rockslides　　(d) blizzards

6. **Picture the island of Surtsey shortly after it formed. What don't you see?**

    (a) lava　　(c) steam

    (b) water　　(d) soil

7. **Would you like to explore the Mid-Ocean Ridge? Explain.**

    _____

    _____

    _____

Science Standard: Understands how species depend on one another and on the environment for survival

Benchmark: Knows that changes in the environment can have different effects on different organisms

Changing with the Environment

Every plant and animal is designed to live in a specific environment, or biome. A cactus would die in a swamp, just as a cattail would die in a desert. These plants are meant to live in different biomes. The cattails grow in the swamp because they need standing water. The cactus likes the high heat and little rainfall of a desert. It stores water inside itself.

Sometimes the environment changes. Then the plants and animals that are suited only to a specific place are suddenly in trouble. They must change in order to survive. Many people believe that a change in environment explains what happened to the dinosaurs. The theory states that a meteor struck Earth millions of years ago and caused a climate change. The world immediately got a lot colder. The cold-blooded dinosaurs needed more heat. They ate the kinds of plants that grew in warm places. The change was too sudden. The dinosaurs couldn't adapt. They all died out.

For the dinosaurs all we have is a theory. Now we have seen other plants and animals die out when the environment changes. Some species can adapt, or change, quickly in response to changes humans make to their environment. One example happened in Britain with the peppered moth. During the early 1800s most peppered moths were white with black spots. Only a few odd ones were black. The white moths blended in with tree trunks. The black ones could easily be seen. Since the birds usually ate them, they did not get to reproduce. The population of white peppered moths stayed large; the population of black peppered moths stayed very small. Then in the mid 1800s people built a lot of factories. The factories' smokestacks sent lots of ashes into the air. These ashes darkened the bark on the trees where the moths lived. Now the white moths no longer blended in with the tree trunks. As a result, the birds saw and ate them. They did not get to reproduce. The number of white peppered moths **dwindled**. More and more black peppered moths survived. Today, most peppered moths in Britain are black.

Unfortunately, most plants and animals cannot adapt so quickly. Many species have become extinct. More die off each day. This is especially true in rainforests, where creatures rarely adapt to a change in their environments.

Changing with the Environment

Comprehension Questions

1. **The dinosaurs may have died because of**

    ⓐ a lack of medicine.

    ⓑ a climate change.

    ⓒ a biome.

    ⓓ a theory.

2. **On a historical time line, what happened second?**

    ⓐ Most peppered moths were black.

    ⓑ Most peppered moths were white.

    ⓒ Factories were built in Britain.

    ⓓ The peppered moth population started to change.

3. **Which is an example of people making a big change to a biome?**

    ⓐ growing a crop   ⓒ opening a beach

    ⓑ filling in a swamp   ⓓ repairing a road

4. **A synonym for *dwindled* is**

    ⓐ darkened.   ⓒ increased.

    ⓑ lightened.   ⓓ decreased.

5. **Which is a biome?**

    ⓐ the temperature   ⓒ the ocean

    ⓑ the sky   ⓓ the sun

6. **Picture a bird searching for peppered moths. Where is it looking?**

    ⓐ on tree trunks   ⓒ under the dirt

    ⓑ in the grass   ⓓ high in the sky

7. **What environmental change do you think would be the easiest for an animal to adapt to: temperature, length of seasons, amount of water available, or kinds of food available? Explain.**

    _____

    _____

    _____

Science Standard: Understands basic Earth processes

Benchmark: Knows how features on the Earth's surface are constantly changed by a combination of slow and rapid processes (e.g. weathering; erosion; and deposition of sediment caused by waves, wind, water, and ice)

Niagara Falls: A Changing Natural Wonder

Niagara Falls is a beautiful part of the Niagara River. This river is part of what separates the U.S. and Canada. Niagara Falls has two parts: the Horseshoe Falls and the American Falls. Canada owns the U-shaped Horseshoe Falls. The American Falls belongs to the U.S. More water goes over Niagara than any other falls in the world. Millions of people visit there each year.

Niagara Falls started out as river rapids. Over time the rushing water wore away the rock of the riverbed. Different kinds of rock erode at different rates. Hard dolomite covered soft layers of limestone, sandstone, and shale. The rushing water tore away the softer rock. The hard layer was left sticking out like a shelf. Water fell over this shelf. The Falls were born!

Twelve thousand years ago Niagara Falls was seven miles (11 km) downstream. Every year more rock wore away. This made the falls move back about three feet (1 m) each year. Slowly the falls moved upstream. This left behind a deep gorge.

During the early 1900s people started **diverting** water from the river above the falls. This water flows into a power plant and makes electricity. The water is released back into the Niagara River below the falls. As the demand for electrical power has increased, more water has been taken. Less water going over the falls means less erosion. So the falls keep moving today, but not as fast as before. Each year the American Falls moves back about an inch (2.5 cm). Lots more water goes over the Horseshoe Falls. It erodes at least 3 inches (8 cm) per year.

Right below the Falls the water has worn a hole as deep as the falls is high! When the lower rock layers wear away enough, the upper ledge will fall. This can be dangerous. Scientists keep track of the Falls' edges. They blast away unstable edges. This way people won't be standing on them when they fall.

Niagara Falls: A Changing Natural Wonder

Comprehension Questions

1. **Niagara Falls was caused by**

   (a) diverting water.

   (b) a deep gorge.

   (c) making electricity.

   (d) water erosion.

2. **On a historical time line, what happened most recently?**

   (a) A gorge formed.

   (b) River rapids caused erosion.

   (c) The Falls erosion decreased.

   (d) The Falls moved upstream.

3. **Why has the Falls' rate of erosion changed?**

   (a) The Falls have reached a layer of very hard rock.

   (b) People have decreased the amount of water that flows over the brink.

   (c) People have built up the brink with cement.

   (d) People have blasted away unstable edges.

4. ***Diverting* means**

   (a) redirecting.

   (b) using.

   (c) changing.

   (d) polluting.

5. **What formed the deep hole beneath the Horseshoe Falls?**

   (a) power shovels

   (b) erosion

   (c) electricity

   (d) explosions

6. **Picture yourself standing right near the brink of Niagara Falls. What don't you see?**

   (a) rapids

   (b) falling water

   (c) swimmers

   (d) rocks

7. **Would you like to visit Niagara Falls? Explain.**

   _____

   _____

   _____

Science Standard: Understands basic Earth processes

Benchmark: Knows how features on the Earth's surface are constantly changed by a combination of slow and rapid processes (e.g. weathering; erosion; and deposition of sediment caused by waves, wind, water, and ice)

The Amazing World Beneath Our Feet

Whenever rain falls, it hits buildings, sidewalks, and roads. Some of it lands in ponds and streams. Most of it ends up on the ground. The raindrops trickle down through the grass and soil. The water picks up carbon from decaying leaves and plants, making it acidic. In some places the water seeps down until it reaches a layer of rock as big as a mountain. The water drips into little cracks and holes in the large rock. Over millions of years and billions of rainstorms, the water gradually wears away these rocks in a process called erosion. Erosion happens when tiny pieces of rock **dissolve** or crumble. After a very long time this makes the cracks and holes get so large that they turn into tunnels and spaces inside the rocks. We call these underground tunnels and spaces limestone caverns. Some of these caves have gigantic rooms and tunnels that can hold many people. Others have deep, narrow passages that no one can enter.

Scientists think that there may be 50,000 limestone caverns in North America, but very few have been found. You can go into some of these caves for an admission fee. People have put electrical wires inside these caves. All other caves have total darkness. As a result most of the animals that live inside caves are blind.

Caverns maintain a constant temperature of about 50ºF (10ºC). They stay cool and damp, since water continues to seep in. Each water drop carries minerals from the rocks it flowed through to reach the cave ceiling. As each drop evaporates, it leaves behind these minerals. The minerals build up. Over a long period of time, rocks that look like icicles form on the cave's ceiling. These "icicles" are called stalactites. As a stalactite drips, a stalagmite may build up beneath it. Stalagmites form from the minerals in the water falling from above. They rise up from the cavern floor, like upside down ice cream cones. It takes 400 years for a stalactite to add one inch (2.5 cm) in length. If a stalactite and a stalagmite meet, they form a column.

There are other kinds of caves, too. Some form when volcanoes erupt. Others form after wind, rain, and snow carves them into the sides of mountains. Caves also form along the coast where the ocean waves cut into the rocks on shore. People have already discovered most of these caves.

The Amazing World Beneath Our Feet

Comprehension Questions

1. **Some people think North America has**

   (a) 500 limestone caverns.   (c) 50,000 limestone caverns.

   (b) 5,000 limestone caverns.   (d) 500,000 limestone caverns.

2. **In the formation of a cave, what happened second?**

   (a) The water turned acidic.

   (b) Rain water seeped down through dead plant matter.

   (c) Water erosion caused cracks in enormous rocks.

   (d) Rooms and tunnels formed.

3. **Which cannot form a cave?**

   (a) volcanic eruptions   (c) wind

   (b) intense heat   (d) water

4. **A synonym for *dissolve* is**

   (a) sink.   (c) melt.

   (b) burn.   (d) harden.

5. **Inside a cave,**

   (a) bats and blind fish may live.

   (b) many different types of plants live.

   (c) plants or animals cannot live.

   (d) sunlight shines through cracks in the rocks.

6. **Picture standing inside a lighted limestone cave. What is on the floor?**

   (a) ferns that need very little light in order to grow

   (b) soil

   (c) stalactites

   (d) stalagmites

7. **Would you like to be the first to explore a limestone cavern? Explain.**

   _____

   _____

   _____

Science Standard: Knows the general structure and functions of cells in organisms

Benchmark: Knows that each plant or animal has different structures which serve different functions in growth, survival, and reproduction

Your Remarkable Body

Your body is an amazing machine. Just as a machine's many parts work together to make it run, your body systems work together to keep you going. These systems include the skeletal system and the muscle system.

All of the bones in your body make up your skeletal system. Bones meet at joints. Moveable joints, like those in the fingers, let the body move. Fixed joints, like those found in the skull, do not let the bones move. Your teeth are bones with a very specific job: chewing food. The other bones form a frame that supports your body and protects its internal organs. Bones do several other tasks, too. Some bone cells take calcium out of the blood and add it to the bone. Calcium makes the bones strong so that they will not break easily. The soft inner part of a bone, called bone marrow, makes and releases new blood cells. The most obvious job that bones do is work with your muscles to let you move.

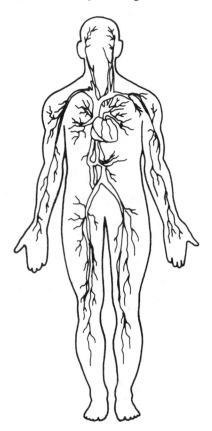

Your muscle system lets your body move and allows your internal organs to work. You have skeletal muscles and smooth muscles. Skeletal muscles move bones and are voluntary muscles that you can control. These muscles move by pulling. Each muscle can only pull in one direction. One end of each skeletal muscle connects to a bone. This bone does not move when the muscle pulls. The other end of that muscle attaches to another bone. This bone does move when the muscle pulls. One set of muscles pulls the bones in one direction; the other set pulls the bone in the other direction. This means that you use one set of muscles to lift your arm up and another set of muscles to move it back down.

Smooth muscles make up most of the body's internal organs. Smooth muscles move food through the digestive system, air through the lungs, and blood through veins and arteries. Since you cannot control these muscles, they're called involuntary muscles. Smooth muscles cannot move as fast as skeletal muscles, but they work **continuously**. Your heart is a smooth muscle. It beats about 75 times each minute, and it will never rest as long as you live.

Your Remarkable Body

Comprehension Questions

1. **You have control of the movement of**

   (a) some of your body's muscles.

   (b) all of your body's muscles.

   (c) none of your body's muscles.

   (d) just your arm and leg muscles.

2. **While you are young, the part of the skeletal system that has its bones replaced by brand new bones is**

   (a) the skull.
   (c) the teeth.

   (b) the feet.
   (d) the hands.

3. **Which is an example of voluntary muscles?**

   (a) your lungs breathing

   (b) your heart beating

   (c) your legs walking

   (d) your intestines digesting food

4. **Another word for *continuously* is**

   (a) rarely.
   (c) rapidly.

   (b) often.
   (d) constantly.

5. **When you break an arm bone, which of these systems is affected?**

   (a) the voluntary muscle system

   (b) the involuntary muscle system

   (c) the respiratory system

   (d) the digestive system

6. **Picture a skeleton. Where do you see moveable joints?**

   (a) in the skull
   (c) in the ribs

   (b) in the knee
   (d) in the teeth

7. **Which body system do you find the most interesting? Explain.**

   _____

   _____

   _____

Science Standard: Understands basic features of Earth

Benchmark: Knows ways in which clouds affect weather and climate

Wild Weather

You've probably heard the saying, "It's raining cats and dogs!" That's just an expression to say that it's raining hard. But would you believe that one day in France it really rained frogs?

It started out just a typical rainy day in a small town near Paris. People went out with raincoats and umbrellas. Everything seemed normal. Suddenly, frogs started falling from the sky. They smashed through car windows. They bounced off people's heads. Everyone was scared. What was happening?

Scientists believe a waterspout made the frogs fall. Waterspouts are like tornadoes that form over large lakes or oceans. A waterspout forms when warm, moist air meets cold, dry air and creates a thick, spinning cloud. This cloud has wind speeds of about 50 miles per hour (80 kph). It can reach up to four miles (6.4 km) high in the atmosphere. Just like a land tornado, a waterspout lifts things up and swirls them around, sometimes dropping them far away. A waterspout lasts longer than a tornado, but it loses power as it moves over land. As its strength **diminishes**, the things it sucked up from the water drop to the ground—sometimes up to 100 miles (160 k) away from where they were collected.

Most waterspouts occur in the tropics, but America has had its share of them. Snails fell in Pennsylvania in 1869. Seven years later, hundreds of large snakes fell in Tennessee. In Louisiana thousands of fish plunged to the ground in 1949. In more recent years a waterspout picked up a five-ton (4.5 metric tons) houseboat and flung it on the ground in Florida.

Wild Weather

Comprehension Questions

1. **Snakes fell from the sky in**

   (a) Louisiana.

   (b) Pennsylvania.

   (c) Tennessee.

   (d) Florida.

2. **In the formation of a waterspout, what would happen third?**

   (a) Water animals are snatched up out of the water.

   (b) Warm air and cold air meet over water.

   (c) A spinning funnel cloud forms.

   (d) Animals fall from the sky.

3. **How do tornadoes and waterspouts differ?**

   (a) The winds in waterspouts spin faster than those in tornadoes.

   (b) Waterspouts can't move over land; tornadoes can.

   (c) Tornadoes cause less damage than waterspouts.

   (d) Tornadoes don't form over water; waterspouts do.

4. **The opposite of *diminishes* is**

   (a) changes.

   (b) fades.

   (c) increases.

   (d) decreases.

5. **Even with modern weather forecasting,**

   (a) no one can predict when a waterspout will occur.

   (b) no one has ever seen a waterspout.

   (c) no one knows how waterspouts form.

   (d) no one knows when a waterspout has happened.

6. **Picture a waterspout over the ocean. What is it most likely to suck up?**

   (a) frogs

   (b) fish

   (c) snails

   (d) snakes

7. **Would you like to experience a waterspout? Explain.**

   _____

   _____

   _____

Science Standard: Understands the scientific enterprise

Benchmark: Knows that people of all ages, backgrounds, and groups have made contributions to science and technology throughout history

A Man Concerned with Safety

Garrett Morgan was born in 1877 to a former slave. When he reached 14, he needed to help support his family. So he left school to work as a handyman. Later he fixed sewing machines. Although he only completed sixth grade, he invented two important things still used today. In fact, one of his inventions helps to keep you safe every day.

In 1914 Morgan made the first gas mask. He called it a safety hood. Its tight canvas hood had a breathing tube that hung to the ground. This let a person breathe clean air even in the midst of deadly fumes. He showed his invention to several companies. Because he was black, no one believed it would really work. Then in 1916 an explosion in a tunnel 282 feet (85.5 m) below Cleveland showed the value of Morgan's invention. Smoke, dust, and natural gas fumes killed several firefighters who tried to get to the men trapped below. Even though the workers were still alive, their situation looked hopeless. No one could go into the tunnel to help them escape.

Morgan heard about the accident. He rushed to the scene. He and his brother Frank put on gas masks. They went down into the tunnel. Together they saved 32 workers' lives. The publicity was just what Morgan needed. Orders poured in for gas masks. A few years later American soldiers used gas masks during World War I. Over time gas masks became standard equipment for soldiers, firefighters, and police officers.

One day Morgan saw a bad crash at a city **intersection**. It really upset him. He wanted to keep other people from dying. But how? There just weren't enough police to direct traffic at every busy intersection. Morgan thought and thought. Then he designed the first traffic light in 1923. He later sold his rights to this invention to General Electric Company. Morgan's light looked different from today's traffic signal. It had only a red and a green signal. But his basic design still directs our traffic. The city of Cleveland gave Morgan a gold medal for all he did to improve public safety.

A Man Concerned with Safety

Comprehension Questions

1. Garrett Morgan invented

(a) gold medals.

(b) traffic lights.

(c) intersections.

(d) mining tunnels.

2. On a historical time line, what happened second?

(a) Morgan designed a gas mask.

(b) Morgan received a medal from the city of Cleveland.

(c) Morgan rescued some miners.

(d) Morgan sold General Electric the rights to his traffic signal.

3. When did Garrett Morgan's fortune change for the better?

(a) after he helped to save 32 men trapped underground

(b) once he started fixing sewing machines

(c) as soon as he invented the safety hood

(d) after he saw a bad car crash

4. At an *intersection*,

(a) two countries share a border.

(b) there is a traffic circle.

(c) people disagree on which way to turn.

(d) two or more roads meet.

5. How did Garrett Morgan's safety hood help people?

(a) It kept them free from burns.

(b) It gave them fresh oxygen from a tank.

(c) It kept them from breathing dangerous fumes.

(d) It prevented car crashes.

6. Picture the trapped workers when they see Garrett and Frank Morgan. What is the look on the workers' faces?

(a) surprise

(b) anger

(c) disappointment

(d) boredom

7. Which of Morgan's inventions was the most important? Explain.

_____

_____

_____

Geography Standard: Understands the changes that occur in the meaning, use, distribution, and importance of resources

Benchmark: Knows the advantages and disadvantages of recycling and reusing different types of materials

Nature's Recycling

Did you know that dead leaves, grass clippings, and fruit and vegetable peels are valuable natural resources? Rather than throw these things in the trash, we can put them to good use in a compost pile. Composting is nature's recycling method. It is a simple way to reuse plant waste. Composting breaks down plant materials into minerals and returns them to the soil. Adding composted soil to a garden helps to grow stronger, healthier plants. Composting keeps plant waste out of trash dumps. Some cities compost on a large scale in order to stop organic materials from taking up space in landfills.

Making your own compost is easy. You gather "food" for bacteria and fungi, then let them do the job. Choose an **inconspicuous** spot in your yard. Place a wood or wire bin there. It doesn't need a lid. That way, when it rains, the pile will get wet. Water helps the materials to decay. Throw kitchen scraps—things like tea bags, orange rinds, and potato peels—into the pile. When you cut your grass, add the clippings to the pile. As a general rule, you can add any brown or green plant matter. Although you can put in eggshells, never add animal droppings, cheese, or pieces of meat or fat. These things take a long time to break down and may attract wild animals.

About twice a month, you must turn the pile by digging it up a bit with a shovel. This way the rotting materials get more air. Many of the bacteria and fungi that break down materials cannot live without enough air. After just one year the compost pile will be smaller and will look like soil. This material is called humus. Humus contains carbon dioxide, calcium, phosphorus, and many other minerals. Spread the humus on your garden, and watch your plants grow. After they die, add them to the compost pile. Then you can recycle those minerals again!

Nature's Recycling

Comprehension Questions

1. **The material made in a compost pile is called**

   (a) clay.

   (b) humus.

   (c) calcium.

   (d) phosphorous.

2. **Read each of the statements below. What would happen third?**

   (a) City workers compost organic materials.

   (b) The city uses humus in the flowerbeds at public parks.

   (c) A truck picks up organic trash.

   (d) People put grass clippings, leaves, and branches by the curb.

3. **Which would be good to add to a compost pile?**

   (a) pieces of fat cut off a pork chop

   (b) a yogurt cup

   (c) banana peel

   (d) bits of Swiss cheese

4. ***Inconspicuous* means**

   (a) not obvious.

   (b) dry.

   (c) dark.

   (d) bright.

5. **Why does a compost pile need turning?**

   (a) so that it won't smell so bad

   (b) so you can reach the humus

   (c) so that it looks better

   (d) so that the material will rot properly

6. **Picture a well-managed compost pile. What don't you see in it?**

   (a) carrot peels

   (b) rotten meat

   (c) eggshells

   (d) grass clippings

7. **When you are an adult, will you do composting? Explain.**

   _____

   _____

   _____

Geography Standard: Understands how physical systems affect human systems

Benchmark: Knows the ways in which human activities are constrained by the physical environment

El Niño Brings Weird Weather

Did you know that a change in the water temperature near South America can affect your weather? It's true. An ocean current runs along the shore of Peru. It normally flows from south to north. Each year in late December it changes direction and flows north to south. When that happens, warmer waters flow along the coast. Sometimes when this happens, the water gets too warm for the fish. They must leave the area to find food. This causes problems for the people in Peru who rely on the fish for food. Without the fish, many seabirds starve. Their bodies fall into the ocean and rot. This makes a chemical called hydrogen sulfide. This chemical combines with the salt in the water to form an acid so strong that it removes the paint on boats. The wind carries this acid through the air and ruins the paint of the houses on shore, too. It also damages crops and other plants. The people of Peru call this event El Niño, Spanish for "little child."

During the 1800s, scientists studied the personal journals of people who lived in Peru hundreds of years ago. They wrote about these **mysterious** events. Their diaries helped scientists to figure out some of their questions about this strange change in the ocean. In the early 1900s Sir Gilbert Walker wanted to predict dangerous monsoons. Monsoons are strong storms that bring wet, warm weather to India each year. Walker did research and found that El Niño caused the weather to change in India. But no one believed him.

It took another 50 years for scientists to really understand that a strong El Niño current near Peru meant weak monsoons on the other side of the world in India. A weak El Niño current meant strong monsoons. In the years when El Niño is especially strong or the current lasts a long time, it can cause weird weather all around the world. This happens because the current changes the location of the warmest ocean waters. Powerful thunderstorms develop over the warmest water. These storms determine where the winds blow. El Niño can cause areas that usually have little rain to get lots of it. Places that need rain for crops may have a bad dry spell.

Most scientists think that a strong El Niño comes every three to seven years. So far no one can really predict which years the current will have the most effect. When the El Niño current is strong, its effects can last up to a year. During the past 40 years the people who study weather have recorded 10 strong El Niños.

El Niño Brings Weird Weather

Comprehension Questions

1. **Strong El Niños usually occur**

   (a) once a decade.

   (b) every year.

   (c) once a century.

   (d) every 3–7 years.

2. **During a year with a strong El Niño, what would happen second?**

   (a) Dead birds fall into the ocean.

   (b) Many fish leave the area.

   (c) The current changes direction.

   (d) Hydrogen sulfide and salt water make a strong acid.

3. **A weak El Niño causes**

   (a) more rain to fall in India.

   (b) less rain to fall in India.

   (c) forest fires in the U.S. Midwest.

   (d) floods in the African deserts.

4. *Mysterious* **means**

   (a) dangerous.

   (b) exciting.

   (c) not understood.

   (d) predictable.

5. **What do you think most Peruvian fishermen do during strong El Niño seasons?**

   (a) They have a celebration.

   (b) They starve to death.

   (c) They stop fishing and start farming.

   (d) They go farther away from home to catch fish.

6. **Picture a monsoon approaching the coast of India. What don't you see?**

   (a) pleasure boats

   (b) flooding

   (c) heavy rainfall

   (d) lightning

7. **What is your favorite type of weather? Explain.**

   _____

   _____

   _____

Geography Standard: Understands the charactertistics of ecosystems on Earth's surface

Benchmark: Knows the components of ecosystems and how human intervention can change them

Staying in Balance

An ecosystem is a community of plants and animals. They interact with each other and their environment. Since ecosystems are based on food chains, an ecosystem must stay in balance. This means that the number of plants and animals stay pretty much the same. Why? Well, if there are too many plant consumers, they will ruin the plant population by eating the plants faster than the plants can grow back. If there are too many animal consumers, they will run out of food.

Suppose a disease killed a lot of birds. The dead birds fall to the ground and rot. Bacteria feed on the dead birds until the number of bacteria is too large. Too many bacteria in the soil cause plants to die. Then mice (plant consumers) can't find enough food. They leave the area or starve. Now the snakes (animal consumers) that ate the mice are left without food. They too must leave the area or starve. The ecosystem's **imbalance** ruined the community.

Unfortunately, people often do things that disrupt the balance of ecosystems. People build houses and roads on land that animals need for homes. They fill in wetlands. They pollute the air, land, and water. Some animals have been hunted almost to extinction.

If humans do not interfere, ecosystems will eventually rebalance on their own. This takes many years. What happened on Isle Royale in Lake Superior is a good example. In the 1920s a pair of moose swam out to Isle Royale. They were the only large animals

there, so by 1930 their population had grown to 3,000! That many moose ate the plants faster than the plants could grow back. In 1933 the moose began to starve. As they died, their numbers dropped. With fewer moose, the plants grew back. Over time the moose population grew again.

In 1950 a pair of wolves swam out to the island. They ate the moose, and the number of wolves increased. When there got to be too many wolves, they started to starve. After many years a stable balance of 600 moose and 20 wolves lived on Isle Royale. There were just enough moose and just enough wolves to keep them both from starving.

Staying in Balance

Comprehension Questions

1. In what year did the moose start to die?

ⓐ 1920   ⓒ 1933

ⓑ 1930   ⓓ 1950

2. On a historical time line, what happened third?

ⓐ Moose came to Isle Royale.

ⓑ Wolves came to Isle Royale.

ⓒ The moose didn't find enough to eat.

ⓓ The wolves didn't have enough to eat.

3. Which human activity would have the biggest effect on an ecosystem?

ⓐ paddling a canoe   ⓒ flying a plane

ⓑ building a campfire   ⓓ building a road in a jungle

4. *Imbalance* means

ⓐ perfection.   ⓒ disharmony.

ⓑ size.   ⓓ dirtiness.

5. What could happen if Isle Royale had 400 moose and 25 wolves?

ⓐ The number of wolves would increase.   ⓒ The number of moose would increase.

ⓑ The moose would eat too many plants.   ⓓ The wolves would begin to starve.

6. Picture a place with so many deer that they are starving. To rebalance the ecosystem, people may

ⓐ try to scare the deer away.

ⓑ allow deer hunting.

ⓒ put out food for the starving deer.

ⓓ pass laws to protect deers from hunters.

7. Would making a new landfill affect the ecosystem of that area? Explain.

_____

_____

_____

Geography Standard: Understands how human actions modify the physical environment

Benchmark: Knows ways in which the physical envionment is stressed by human activities

Changing the Chinchilla

Chinchillas are small mammals that once lived wild in the Andes Mountains in South America. A chinchilla has a bushy tail and a rabbit-like face but with shorter, rounder ears. It eats tree bark, roots, and dry grass. Gnawing these things trims its sharp teeth. Like all rodents, a chinchilla's teeth grow daily, so constant chewing keeps the teeth the right length.

When the Europeans came to South America, they discovered the chinchilla. They noticed its thick, soft, gray fur. Soon this fur became highly prized for making coats for the richest people in Europe. Since it took 120 to 150 chinchillas to make one coat, this was bad news for these animals. By 1919 they were nearly extinct.

One day a man walked into a mining camp carrying a young chinchilla in a tin can. An American, Mathias Chapman, bought the little animal and named him Pete. Chapman knew that chinchilla fur was rare and valuable. He decided to bring a group of chinchillas back to America to start a fur ranch. He went home and got three men to come and help him trap them. Since chinchillas sleep all day and look for food at night, catching them was a challenge. And there were so few chinchillas left that after three years they had only found 11! In 1923 Chapman brought the animals to California and started to breed them. It took a long time to build a herd. Unlike most rodents, chinchillas have just one to three babies at a time. They also have babies only two or three times a year.

Finally Chapman's herd grew big enough that he had a few chinchillas to sell. Others came to buy his animals and start their own ranches. They saw Pete riding on Chapman's shoulder. One of them had a new idea: selling chinchillas as pets.

Today there are millions of chinchillas all over the world living on fur ranches or as people's pets. Just like we have cows, horses, and dogs, humans have changed chinchillas into **domesticated** animals. Few are ever seen in the Andes Mountains. No one knows for certain how many wild chinchillas still exist. Laws now protect wild ones from being killed.

Changing the Chinchilla

Comprehension Questions

1. **Why were chinchillas near to extinction?**

   (a) People wanted their ivory.

   (b) People wanted their fur.

   (c) People wanted their meat.

   (d) People wanted them for medical research.

2. **On a historical time line, what happened second?**

   (a) Europeans discovered chinchilla fur.

   (b) Chinchillas lived in the Andes Mountains.

   (c) Mathias Chapman bought a chinchilla.

   (d) Chinchillas lived in fur ranches.

3. **Which of these is not a domesticated animal?**

   (a) a pig   (c) a deer

   (b) a goat   (d) a parakeet

4. *Domesticated* **animals are always**

   (a) farm animals.   (c) valuable.

   (b) kept for human purposes.   (d) cheap.

5. **What probably would have happened if Chapman hadn't caught 11 chinchillas?**

   (a) Chinchillas would have multiplied until there were thousands in the wild.

   (b) Most chinchillas would have died from a disease.

   (c) Chinchillas might have died off completely.

   (d) No one would know what a chinchilla looks like.

6. **Picture yourself looking at a book of mammal photos. What animal's picture won't you see?**

   (a) a bat   (c) a squirrel

   (b) an otter   (d) a goose

7. **Should people raise chinchillas to kill in order to use their fur for coats, collars, and hats? Explain.**

   _____

   _____

   _____

Geography Standard: Understands how human actions modify the physical environment

Benchmark: Knows ways in which the physical envionment is stressed by human activities

The Mighty Redwood

A redwood tree grows taller than any other living thing. The tallest one ever found was the height of a 38-story skyscraper! Yet these giants grow from tiny pine cones less than an inch long. They have short, flat needles. Their deeply grooved, thick bark ranges from red to brown.

Redwood trees can live longer than anything else. So far the oldest one ever cut down was 2,200 years old. Scientists think that they can live for 4,000 years! Their only enemies are windstorms and chainsaws. Disease, insects, and even forest fires do not kill them. Forest fires can reach temperatures of 3,000°F (1,649°C). The tree's bark burns, but its core stays alive. They even survive lightning strikes. After enduring fire or a lightning strike, it takes about 100 years for the bark to grow back. High winds can knock a redwood down, but if the roots stay in the dirt, dozens of new saplings will grow on the spot. A cut stump or broken-off trunk also sends up sprouts. These trees are so hardy that none have died from old age. However, they have a very limited growing area. They need a foggy climate that gets neither too hot nor too cold. They live only in the area between the southern border of Oregon and Big Sur, California.

Redwood trees get their name from their lumber. Their wood is always a clear, light red. It doesn't rot like most woods when exposed to weather. Instead, it turns a darker red. During the California gold rush many homes had to be built quickly. People made homes from redwood lumber. They discovered that it resisted termites and fire. These qualities make redwood a **desirable** building material. As a result, only five percent of the original trees are still standing. Most of the remaining redwoods stand on land owned by lumber companies. To save these trees, a woman named Julia Hill spent more than two years living in the branches of one of these giants. She came

down only after the lumber company agreed to stop cutting down the trees. Today 70,000 acres (28,329 hectares) of redwood forest are public parks.

The Mighty Redwood

1. Most redwood trees have died from

(a) being cut down.

(b) forest fires.

(c) diseases carried by termites.

(d) the damage caused by lightning strikes.

2. What happened last?

(a) Redwood trees grew in a foggy area on the West Coast.

(b) People used redwood lumber during the California gold rush.

(c) Julia Hill spent two years living in a redwood tree.

(d) Lumber companies cut down many acres of redwoods.

3. Why are there so few redwood trees in America?

(a) because they die so easily

(b) because people don't like how they look

(c) because it's illegal to own them

(d) because they can only grow in a very limited area

4. *Desirable* means

(a) sturdy.

(b) wanted.

(c) inexpensive.

(d) unfinished.

5. Why is redwood lumber valuable?

(a) It cannot burn.

(b) It's attractive and doesn't rot.

(c) The trees don't die easily.

(d) The trees are so plentiful.

6. Picture a person standing next to an adult redwood tree. Compared to the tree, the person looks

(a) strong.

(b) old.

(c) large.

(d) tiny.

7. Should all lumber companies be forced to stop cutting down redwood trees? Explain.

_____

_____

_____

Geography Standard: Understands the characteristics of ecosystems on Earth's surface

Benchmark: Knows ways in which humans can change ecosystems

We Need Wetlands

Wetlands are ecosystems found in low, flat areas. Often they border ponds, rivers, lakes, and oceans. Wetlands include marshes, swamps, and bogs. No trees grow in a marsh, but there are lots of grassy plants, such as cattails. They thrive in the soggy ground covered by shallow water. Ducks, swans, turtles, and many different bugs live there, too.

Florida has the world's biggest freshwater marsh. The Everglades covers 4,000 square miles (103,600 sq. km). The Everglades is not entirely fresh water, however. Near the sea the fresh water and salt water mix. Some plants and animals can live only in this brackish water.

Saltwater marshes lie along the East Coast and the Gulf of Mexico. During high tide these marshes are under water. During low tide these marshes are visible. The water rushes out, carrying bits of plants, dead animals, and minerals necessary for sea animals. Many plants and animals depend upon this ever-changing environment.

Many wetlands go through stages. Swamps begin as marshes. If the water covering the marsh gets shallow enough, trees and bushes take root. Swamps have trees that grow with their roots underwater. Usually the water level changes with the amount of rainfall. If the trees' roots stay underwater too long, they die. This leaves ghostly stumps in the murky water. Water snakes, frogs, beaver, heron, and moose are just a few of the animals that live in swamps.

Bogs have damp, spongy soil. So many dead plants have piled up that there is no longer any standing water. This rotting plant matter turns into peat. In Ireland and Scotland peat is dried and burned to heat homes. Bog soil is useful for growing cranberries and wild rice. Salamanders and lots of insects live there.

People have destroyed more than half of the 215 million acres of wetlands that were once in the U.S.* Parts of some major cities—including Washington, D.C.; San Francisco; and Boston—stand on former wetlands. First the swampy land was filled in with truckloads of dirt. Then people put buildings and streets on the new land.

Most people do not find wetlands beautiful. Swamps can have a bad odor, too. But wetlands are important. Marshes and swamps store water, thus reducing the flooding a heavy rain can cause. They **replenish** underground water supplies. The wetland plants keep water from eroding the surrounding land. About one-third of all of America's endangered plants and animals live in these areas. Now laws protect some wetlands. More than a dozen wetlands in the U.S. are refuges and wildlife preserves.

(* *not including Alaska*)

We Need Wetlands

1. **The world's largest freshwater marsh is in**

   (a) Ireland.   (c) Florida.

   (b) Mexico.   (d) Scotland.

2. **Think about how wetlands change over time. What would happen first?**

   (a) Peat is used to heat homes.

   (b) There is a marsh.

   (c) There is a bog.

   (d) There is a swamp.

3. **How do saltwater marshes differ from freshwater marshes?**

   (a) Saltwater marshes change daily; fresh water marshes do not.

   (b) Freshwater marshes change several times daily; salt water marshes do not.

   (c) Saltwater marshes are endangered; fresh water marshes are not.

   (d) Freshwater marshes are endangered; salt water marshes are not.

4. ***Replenish* means**

   (a) to drain.   (c) to open up.

   (b) to clean.   (d) to refill.

5. **From the article you can tell that brackish water is found**

   (a) only in freshwater swamps and marshes.

   (b) only in saltwater marshes.

   (c) where salt and fresh water combine.

   (d) only in bogs.

6. **Picture a swamp. What would you be surprised to see there?**

   (a) rotten logs   (c) ducks

   (b) sea gulls   (d) snapping turtles

7. **Do you think that is it okay to fill in wetlands if the space is needed for new homes in a growing city? Explain.**

   _____

   _____

   _____

History Standard: Understands how European society experienced political, economic, and cultural transformation in an age of global intercommunication between 1450 and 1750

Benchmark: Understands the signficance of the Scientific Revolution and the Age of Enlightenment (e.g., the impact of inventions such as the printing press)

Communicating Then and Now

People have always wanted to share ideas. Even toddlers communicate: they smile, cry, and point. The earliest people moved their hands and grunted to show others what they meant. They drew pictures on cave walls. Over time, people developed spoken language. Language let people share their ideas more easily than grunting, pointing, and drawing.

Communication took another giant leap forward when people began to write. Written language let people who could read and write share ideas with each other. Many ancient **cultures** came up with different ways to write. The Egyptians used *hieroglyphs*, or pictures. Each picture stood for a sound. People in Western Asia carved marks into clay. They called these marks *cuneiforms*. The Chinese and Japanese still use their ancient symbol systems. Every word has a unique symbol that must be memorized. We use a 26-letter alphabet. We arrange these letters into patterns that make different words. Today, we write words in notes, reports, and e-mail messages.

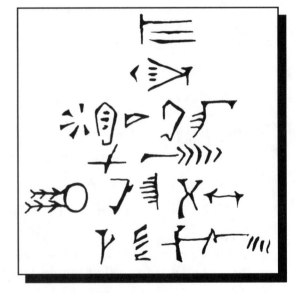

Long ago very few people knew how to read or write. Books were handwritten, not published. This meant that every copy of a book had to be copied by hand. Monks spent their entire lives copying the Bible over and over again. It took them years to make just one copy. Then in 1520 Johannes Gutenberg invented the printing press. The printing press let information be set in type—metal pieces with letters on them. The type was inked and pressed onto paper. In this way, many copies could be made of the same page.

Since then billions of books, magazines, and newspapers have been printed, giving many people the chance to read the same ideas. Now the Internet lets us read things from all over the world. Every day there is more information available to us.

Communicating Then and Now

Comprehension Questions

1. **Who used a specific symbol for each word in the language?**

   (a) the Chinese   (c) the monks

   (b) the Egyptians   (d) Gutenberg

2. **On a historical time line, what happened second?**

   (a) People wrote with an alphabet.

   (b) People wrote with hieroglyphs.

   (c) Monks copied the Bible.

   (d) Many people spoke the same language.

3. **During the time when few people could read or write,**

   (a) most people learned a lot of math instead.

   (b) everyone knew how to sign his or her own name.

   (c) most people learned by experience and oral explanations.

   (d) history was recorded with great accuracy and detail.

4. ***Cultures* are**

   (a) countries.   (c) societies.

   (b) languages.   (d) families.

5. **Today**

   (a) everyone has adopted a common alphabet for writing.

   (b) everyone in the world learns to read and write a language.

   (c) less people know how to read and write than ever before.

   (d) more people know how to read and write than ever before.

6. **Picture the monks copying the Bible. What are they using?**

   (a) a pencil   (c) a marker

   (b) a feather pen and ink pot   (d) a paintbrush

7. **What is your favorite way to communicate with someone far away? Explain.**

   _____

   _____

   _____

History Standard: Understands the economic boom and social transformation of post-World War II United States

Benchmark: Understands the impact of postwar scientific research on contemporary society

Visiting the Moon

During his term in office, President Kennedy gave full funding to NASA, the space agency. He did this because he wanted to see Americans land on the moon. In July 1969 three men fulfilled Kennedy's dream during the Apollo 11 mission. Thousands of people had worked for years in order to send them to the moon. There had been 10 prior Apollo missions. One had failed, but the others were successful. Finally it was time to try a moon landing.

Their spacecraft took off from NASA in Houston, Texas. A Saturn 5 rocket carried the astronauts and their spacecraft into orbit. They blasted through space at speeds as fast as 25,000 miles per hour (40,234 kph). Even at that incredible speed, it took four days to reach the moon. The men had a special craft designed only for landing on the moon. This **lunar** module was called the *Eagle*.

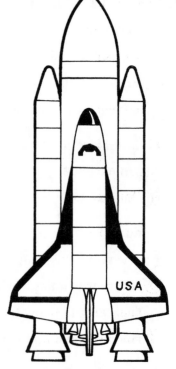

After the *Eagle* landed, Neil Armstrong stepped out onto the moon. People all over the world watched on their television sets as he said, "That's one small step for man, one giant leap for mankind." Buzz Aldrin followed Armstrong onto the moon's surface, but Michael Collins stayed circling the moon in the main spacecraft. He had to make sure that nothing happened to the spacecraft that would take them home.

The astronauts moved around on the moon, gathering rocks and taking photographs. They did many experiments on the moon. Before they left, they planted an American flag in the ground in the place where they landed. Next to it they put a plaque that read, "We came in peace for all mankind." The flag and the plaque are still there.

Some people think that moon travel may become common. They want to build hotels on the moon and have people go on lunar vacations! If that happens, people will visit the site of the first moon landing. They will stand where Neil Armstrong made history.

Visiting the Moon

Comprehension Questions

1. **Where did the astronauts put a U.S. flag?**

   (a) on the lunar buggy   (c) on the Saturn 5 rocket

   (b) on the moon   (d) on their spacecraft

2. **On a historical time line, what happened first?**

   (a) Astronauts went in the space shuttle.

   (b) Neil Armstrong walked on the moon.

   (c) The Apollo 13 had an emergency.

   (d) President Kennedy gave full funding to NASA.

3. **Neil Armstrong stepping onto the moon is most like**

   (a) Isaac Newton naming the laws of motion.

   (b) Christopher Columbus discovering North America.

   (c) Roald Amundsen reaching the South Pole before anyone else.

   (d) Gutenberg inventing the printing press.

4. **The word *lunar* means**

   (a) "of the moon."   (c) "of an astronaut."

   (b) "of the sun."   (d) "of an eagle."

5. **What did Armstrong mean by, "…one giant leap for mankind"?**

   (a) that it was a really big step down from the spacecraft

   (b) that it was a moment of major progress for a human to step onto the moon

   (c) that only men should go to the moon

   (d) that he could do big leaps on the moon because of its low gravity

6. **Picture standing on the surface of the moon. The most colorful thing you see is**

   (a) the rocks.   (c) the sunset.

   (b) the plants.   (d) the American flag.

7. **Would you like to vacation on the moon? Explain.**

   _____

   _____

   _____

History Standard: Understands the causes and course of World War II, the character of the war at home and abroad, and its reshaping of the U.S. role in world affairs

Benchmark: Understands significant military aspects of world War II

World War II Submarines

America entered World War II after the Japanese attacked Pearl Harbor. Since the attack was a complete surprise, it wrecked most of the American warships there.

Japan is an island in the Pacific Ocean. It has few natural resources. All of its fuel came by ship. So did all the materials needed to build planes, ships, and submarines for the war.

Of course, Americans did not want the Japanese to get fuel or supplies. Yet for the first months of the war, the U.S. only had submarines that were able to fight. So the subs were sent to sink the ships carrying goods to Japan. They did an amazing job. Even though subs had less than 2% of the Navy's **manpower**, they caused more than half of Japan's shipping losses: 5.3 million tons of materials and fuel.

U.S. subs also gathered information. Later in the war, they rescued American pilots who had their planes shot down over the ocean. The first President George Bush was one of the Navy pilots saved in this way.

Life on a submarine was not easy. The air was stuffy. It was crowded. There was no place to be alone. In the main aisle of the sub, each man had to frequently pause while

someone squeezed past. Each person's bunk was barely big enough to lie down on. Serving on a sub was scary, too. If an enemy discovered a sub, the sailors had to shut down its engines and hope that the depth charges fired on them would miss.

Due to the many hardships, everyone on a sub was a volunteer. Before going down, these men had to pass a lot of physical and mental testing. They had to convince doctors that they wouldn't crack under the pressure of being thousands of feet below water with no chance for escape or rescue.

Many men on subs lost their lives in World War II. More than 3,600 Americans lie in watery graves where their submarines sank.

World War II Submarines

Comprehension Questions

1. **The Japanese needed supply ships because**

    (a) the ships were so reliable and always delivered all of the goods.

    (b) they didn't have the money to develop their own resources.

    (c) it was cheap to import fuel.

    (d) they didn't have the supplies on their own island.

2. **On a historical time line, what happened second?**

    (a) U.S. subs picked up downed American pilots.

    (b) U.S. subs attacked supply ships.

    (c) The Japanese lost World War II.

    (d) The Japanese attacked Pearl Harbor.

3. **Why are so many submariners on the bottom of the ocean instead of in a cemetery?**

    (a) Their families didn't want their bodies returned to them.

    (b) They asked to be buried at sea.

    (c) It was too difficult to find them and bring them back to the surface.

    (d) People in wars aren't buried; their bodies are left lying wherever they die.

4. *Manpower* **means**

    (a) the number of men minus the number of women.

    (b) something that works when people push it.

    (c) the number of people working.

    (d) having a manual instead of an automatic transmission.

5. **Why did each submariner have to go through so much testing?**

    (a) to be sure the man could stay calm under high stress and fear

    (b) to keep out men who didn't like swimming

    (c) to know which men truly wanted to volunteer

    (d) to keep out men who came from small families

6. **Picture a World War II submarine under water. How can the captain best see what is happening on the surface?**

    (a) only by bringing the submarine up to the surface

    (b) by having some men swim to the surface

    (c) by opening a hatch

    (d) by using a periscope

7. **Would you have volunteered to serve on a World War II submarine? Explain.**

    _____

    _____

    _____

History Standard: Understands reform, revolution, and social change in the world economy of the early 20th century

Benchmark: Understands factors that transformed American and European society in the early 20th century (e.g. major scientific, medical, and technological advances at the turn of the century)

The Sky's the Limit!

When they were kids, Orville and Wilbur Wright loved bicycles. They even built their own bikes. When they grew up, the brothers started a bike repair shop. Years later, they built the world's first successful airplane in that shop.

In 1896 Wilbur read a book about gliders. Gliders are planes without motors. They move by riding air currents. The book said that people wanted to put engines on gliders so that they could go farther. Nobody knew how to build a glider with an engine, but lots of people were trying. Everyone wanted to be the first to invent it.

Wilbur showed the book to Orville. They got excited and decided they would build a flying machine. To get ideas from nature, the brothers spent entire days on a hilltop watching hawks glide on the wind. They read everything they could about gliders and flight. They found that changes in wind speed or direction could make planes crash. So Wilbur came up with a glider that had moveable wings. The glider could tilt its wings to **compensate** for changes in the wind speed or direction.

The brothers built a wind tunnel so that they could test the glider in different winds. When the glider had trouble staying in the air, they modified it again and again to make it work better. When they created their third glider, they added a motor. They flipped a coin to see which of them would get the first chance to fly it. Orville won the toss, and on December 17, 1903, he flew the world's first engine-powered plane in Kitty Hawk, North Carolina. During that 12-second flight, their airplane went only 120 feet (37 m)— but it changed the world of transportation forever.

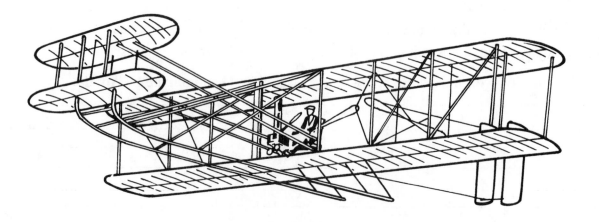

The Sky's the Limit!

Comprehension Questions

1. **Who flew the world's first glider with a motor on December 17, 1903?**

   (a) OrvilleWright

   (b) Wilbur Wright

   (c) Kitty Hawk

   (d) Amelia Earhart

2. **On a historical time line, what happened first?**

   (a) Orville and Wilbur built a wind tunnel.

   (b) Wilbur read a book about gliders.

   (c) The brothers built several gliders.

   (d) The brothers spent hours studying birds in flight.

3. **Why did the Wright brothers test all of their gliders in a wind tunnel?**

   (a) because they needed to know how each glider would react to different winds

   (b) because the glider got its power from the wind

   (c) because wind was necessary to help each glider land

   (d) because they thought it was interesting

4. **A synonym for *compensate* is**

   (a) spin.

   (b) lower.

   (c) raise.

   (d) adjust.

5. **You can tell that Orville and Wilbur**

   (a) wanted to be rich.

   (b) liked to go to school.

   (c) liked to work with their hands.

   (d) had no money.

6. **Picture the Wright brothers watching birds fly. What are the men doing?**

   (a) lying on the grass

   (b) making notes and sketches

   (c) fixing a bike

   (d) making an oil painting

7. **Would you like to learn how to fly? Explain.**

   _____

   _____

   _____

History Standard: Understands how democratic values came to be; and how they have been exemplified by people, events, and symbols

Benchmark: Understands how people over the last 200 years have continued to struggle to bring to all groups in American society the liberties and equality promised in the basic principles of American democracy

Working for the Right to Work

Asa Philip Randolph was a leader in the American civil-rights movement. He worked for more than 40 years to get equal rights for black workers. In the 1920s the men who worked as train porters formed the biggest black labor union. They made Randolph their leader. He got the railroad companies to treat the workers better.

Asa Philip Randolph

During World War II the companies that made war supplies did not treat black workers fairly. They would not give them jobs. Jobs went to white workers even when the black workers had more skills. Once a black man got a job, no matter how hard he worked, he could not move up to a better job. When Randolph found out, he wanted things changed. He went to see President Franklin D. Roosevelt. He asked the president to end the unfair treatment of black workers. But Roosevelt did nothing. Then Randolph said that he would get more than 100,000 blacks to march to the White House. They would protest. Then everyone would know about the problem.

Franklin D. Roosevelt

So Roosevelt decided to act. In June 1941 he signed a law. It stated that a person could not be denied a job due to race, color, religion, or national origin. The law only applied to the government and companies that made war supplies. Yet it was a step in the right direction. The next year the National **Association** for the Advancement of Colored People gave Randolph their highest award.

In 1957 the biggest labor union in the U.S. made Randolph its vice president. In 1963 he organized a march in Washington, D.C. People from all over the country marched. They wanted people to know about the many problems blacks still faced.

Working for the Right to Work

Comprehension Questions

1. **When President Roosevelt signed the bill in 1941, he**

   (a) ended all discrimination against blacks.

   (b) made job discrimination illegal throughout the U.S.A.

   (c) made job discrimination illegal in the government and war supply companies.

   (d) made sure blacks would have better educations.

2. **On a historical time line, what happened third?**

   (a) Randolph led a black labor union.

   (b) Randolph received an award from the National Association for the Advancement of Colored People.

   (c) Randolph visited President Roosevelt.

   (d) Randolph organized a march on Washington, D.C.

3. **Why did the National Association for the Advancement of Colored People give Randolph its highest award?**

   (a) because he organized a march on Washingon, D.C.

   (b) because he was the leader of the biggest black labor union

   (c) because he was the vice president of America's biggest labor union

   (d) because he helped to bring about a law that helped black workers

4. **The meaning of the word *association* is**

   (a) group.   (b) funds.   (c) laws.   (d) changes.

5. **Why did Randolph want to get blacks to march on Washington, D.C.?**

   (a) He wanted to cause trouble for the unions.

   (b) He wanted the nation to know that blacks still faced discrimination.

   (c) He hoped that the march would bring him a lot of fame and money.

   (d) He wanted blacks to have a chance to socialize with each other.

6. **Picture Randolph talking to President Roosevelt. What is the look on Randolph's face?**

   (a) depressed   (b) astonished   (c) determined   (d) joyful

7. **Randolph died in 1979. Do you think he would be pleased with the progress that African Americans have made since his death? Explain.**

   _____

   _____

   _____

History Standard: Understands the United States territorial expansion between 1801 and 1861, and how it affected relations with external powers and Native Americans

Benchmark: Understands the factors that led to U.S. territorial expansion in the Western Hemisphere (e.g., expeditions of American explorers)

Sacagawea Helped to Explore America

When Sacagawea was just 12 years old, Red Arrow kidnapped her. He took her to live with his tribe. Instead of her tipi, she had to live in a dark, earth-covered dome. Every day she worked in the fields. She never left the village until Red Arrow lost her in a bet. A fur trapper named Charbonneau won her. Sacagawea became his third wife. He and his other wives treated her as their slave. No one could guess the important role this young woman would play in U.S. history.

President Jefferson made the Louisiana Purchase in 1803. He asked Lewis and Clark to explore this land west of the Mississippi River. Jefferson hoped that they would find a water route to the Pacific Ocean. Lewis and Clark hired Charbonneau to help them. They asked to take Sacagawea, too. She went along, carrying her newborn baby on her back. Seeing her made Native Americans less afraid of the explorers. They did not attack. Both Lewis and Clark wrote in their journals that they might not have survived their trip to the West Coast without her.

While the men rode in a boat, Sacagawea often walked along the riverbanks, picking plants for food. She asked the Shoshone tribe to give them horses and tell them how to **traverse** the Rocky Mountains. She greeted other Native Americans using a language like their own. She also acted quickly when their boat tipped over. She grabbed their journals, instruments, and medicines before they sank or floated away. She made their 7,500-mile trip a success.

Lewis and Clark's long journey opened the West to white settlers. America started to expand from the East Coast to the West Coast. In Sacagawea's honor, the U.S. put her image on a one-dollar coin.

Sacagawea Helped to Build America

Comprehension Questions

1. Who hired Charbonneau?

(a) President Jefferson   (c) Red Arrow

(b) Sacagawea   (d) Lewis and Clark

2. On a historical time line, what happened second?

(a) Charbonneau married Sacagawea.

(b) Red Arrow kidnapped Sacagawea.

(c) Sacagawea had a baby.

(d) Sacagawea helped Lewis and Clark.

3. How are modern parents like Sacagawea?

(a) They often carry their babies in backpacks.

(b) They take their newborns on long journeys.

(c) They carry their babies through an unknown wilderness.

(d) They search riverbanks for food and medicine.

4. The word *traverse* means

(a) enjoy.   (c) travel across.

(b) find.   (d) go under.

5. What disappointed Jefferson about Lewis and Clark's journey?

(a) They never reached the Pacific Ocean.

(b) They could not find a water route to the West Coast.

(c) When their boat tipped over, they lost all of the maps and journals they had made.

(d) He didn't like the fact that Lewis and Clark had taken Sacagawea along.

6. Picture Lewis and Clark's boat. What don't you see?

(a) oars   (c) a wood frame

(b) sails   (d) paddle wheel

7. Would you have liked to go with Sacagawea on Lewis and Clark's trip? Explain.

_____

_____

_____

Answer Key

Page 9

1. a
2. c
3. d
4. b
5. a
6. d
7. Accept well-supported answers.

Page 11

1. b
2. b
3. d
4. a
5. b
6. d
7. Accept well-supported answers.

Page 13

1. b
2. c
3. b
4. d
5. c
6. a
7. Accept well-supported answers.

Page 15

1. d
2. c
3. b
4. a
5. b
6. c
7. Accept well-supported answers.

Page 17

1. c
2. a
3. b
4. c
5. a
6. d
7. Accept well-supported answers.

Page 19

1. a
2. c
3. c
4. d
5. a
6. b
7. Accept well-supported answers.

Page 21

1. c
2. a
3. d
4. c
5. a
6. b
7. Accept well-supported answers.

Page 23

1. b
2. c
3. a
4. d
5. c
6. a
7. Accept well-supported answers.

Page 25

1. b
2. a
3. c
4. a
5. d
6. b
7. Accept well-supported answers.

Page 27

1. d
2. b
3. a
4. c
5. d
6. a
7. Accept well-supported answers.

Page 29

1. c
2. b
3. d
4. c
5. d
6. b
7. Accept well-supported answers.

Page 31

1. b
2. a
3. c
4. b
5. c
6. d
7. Accept well-supported answers.

Page 33

1. a
2. c
3. d
4. b
5. b
6. d
7. Accept well-supported answers.

Page 35

1. c
2. b
3. a
4. d
5. c
6. b
7. Accept well-supported answers.

Page 37

1. a
2. b
3. c
4. c
5. d
6. b
7. Accept well-supported answers.

Page 39

1. b
2. d
3. c
4. a
5. b
6. d
7. Accept well-supported answers.

Page 41

1. d
2. b
3. c
4. c
5. a
6. d
7. Accept well-supported answers.

Page 43

1. a
2. b
3. a
4. d
5. c
6. b
7. Accept well-supported answers.

Page 45

1. c
2. b
3. d
4. a
5. b
6. c
7. Accept well-supported answers.

Page 47

1. d
2. a
3. a
4. c
5. b
6. d
7. Accept well-supported answers.